Learn ...
How to Acquire

MONEY RICHES and WEALTH

by

Floyd M. Chitalu

AuthorHouse™
1663 Liberty Drive
Bloomington, IN 47403
www.authorhouse.com
Phone: 1-800-839-8640

© 2012 by Floyd M. Chitalu. All rights reserved.

No part of this book may be reproduced, stored in a retrieval system, or transmitted by any means without the written permission of the author.

Published by AuthorHouse   03/24/2012

ISBN: 978-1-4678-9638-2 (sc)
ISBN: 978-1-4678-9639-9 (e)

Any people depicted in stock imagery provided by Thinkstock are models, and such images are being used for illustrative purposes only.
Certain stock imagery © Thinkstock.

This book is printed on acid-free paper.

Because of the dynamic nature of the Internet, any web addresses or links contained in this book may have changed since publication and may no longer be valid. The views expressed in this work are solely those of the author and do not necessarily reflect the views of the publisher, and the publisher hereby disclaims any responsibility for them.

Contents

Chapter 1	Introduction	1
Chapter 2	The beginnings	5
Chapter 3	The Human Brain & the Mind	9
Chapter 4	Learning	13
Chapter 5	Competition	20
Chapter 6	Creativity	24
Chapter 7	Money, Riches and Wealth	27
Chapter 8	Age Conundrum	32
Chapter 9	Sex desire	39
Chapter 10	Capital	44
Chapter 11	What kind of people can acquire more money, riches and wealth?	50
Chapter 12	How to acquire money, riches and Wealth	56
Chapter 13	The Opportunities to make you rich	63
Chapter 14	Setting priorities in your life and living	67
Chapter 15	The Secret Code to getting rich	70
Chapter 16	Conclusion	77

Foreword

To help you decide if you want to continue reading, you may want to know my qualifications for writing the information in this book. I am an intellectual with academic qualifications of Master of Education (M.Ed.), Master of Business Administration (MBA), Bachelor of Science (B.Sc.) Degree in Production Management, Diploma in Crops Production and Diploma in Teaching. I am also a current student in Mathematics and Its Learning.

During my career, I have been a dynamic professional with sound understanding of the configuration of resources for the purposes of production, transport, supply and service functions and have expertise in manpower training & development. I worked as Senior Industrial Engineer, my company internal consultancy job in the copper mining industry where I undertook numerous productivity studies in company operations and formulated strategies and tactics for the implementation of productivity study recommendations. I also worked as part-time lecturer in LCCI Marketing and LCCI Selling & Sales Management and served as secondary school teacher in woodwork and mathematics in the ministry of education.

As an entrepreneur I registered my own company called Wehaveit Company Limited. Under my directorship this trading company established a national network of operations with poise for international business expansion following the company's profitability, stability and growth strides. I am also the Principal Director of a micro-finance enterprise, Fantom Business Services, which is my mode of discourse for training and provision of micro-finance loans for individuals, households, small and medium sized businesses, thereby contributing to the paradigms of financial sustainability, poverty alleviation and empowerment among financially disadvantaged people both in rural and urban locale.

I believe that my accumulated knowledge and wisdom arising from tough tested experiences of my life and living as an individual, family man, employee, self employed, employer and trainer can have the multiplier effect when I communicate to many readers of this book. I invite the readers of my book to push your barriers and take any undertaking they personally engage in and acquire more money, riches and wealth.

Introduction

I have written this book hoping to inspire you to acquire more money, riches and wealth so that you can enjoy your one and only life here on earth to the fullest. I have considered the plain truth that up to ninety percent of people have never deciphered the concept of acquiring sufficient money, riches and wealth they need to live a fuller life. Even though it seems common sense that having sufficient money, riches and wealth can enable anyone enjoy life abundantly, this common sense is not clearly understood by many people. That is the reason why few people get rich whilst the majority do not. I have written my script in as much plain language as possible so that many more common people can read and clearly understand this paradigm.

Acquiring enough money, riches and wealth is not far beyond the capacity of many people and anyone can undoubtedly accumulate lots of money, riches and wealth. Any person has all the basic prerequisites it takes to redirect oneself into great wealth accumulation and it is surely never too late. I want you to realise that you passionately need to take charge of yourself and release the creative power within you to achieve abundant financial and material possessions. You have the capacity to think, you have strength and great potential in you. If you are not yet rich you are most likely the very person restricting yourself and you should blame no one because they too can equally blame you. You can acquire the money, riches and wealth you want if you are ready, determined and focused. I will show you what to do and how to do it by the time you grasp the know-how contained in this book. Success comes to those who are or who become success conscious.

Whatever your age or status, read this book and obtain the secret of how those people who became rich got it right and be inspired to be rich yourself. There is nothing wrong in wanting to get rich and wealthy because the desire for riches is actually the desire for a richer, fuller and more abundant life. It is perfectly right that you should desire to have enough money, riches and wealth. Having enough money, riches and wealth is a privilege that guarantees your financial and economic freedom which will substantially influence your personal mental state and class position in society. The man or woman who does not desire to have enough money to buy all he wants and live more abundantly is abnormal. If you are not abnormal, dare have enough money, riches and wealth and you are rest assured that you will attain a higher standard of living than what you currently enjoy! To be or not to be rich is your idiosyncratic choice you can make, but you are obviously aware that the 'haves' evidently enjoy a high standard of living than the 'have nots'.

The concepts presented in this book will suggest to you that much of what is taught in school education does not, in precise terms, explicitly point out the concept of accumulating money, riches and wealth. It is indeed good to be educated because education empowers you with knowledge and as we all know, knowledge is power. However, the concept of getting rich is a paradigm that does not particularly recognise much the importance of educational attainments. The reality is anyone, both the educated and the uneducated, can become rich.

If you make more money you will have financial freedom and be able to buy whatever you want any time. You will derive greater satisfaction from life, freeing your mind from anger, regret, shame and guilt surrounding your current poor financial status. You will have a feeling of personal fulfilment and self actualisation, the feeling that you can become everything you are capable of becoming in your life time. You must also remember that in your old age when you have fewer people or no one at all willing to help you, the money you will have accumulated will help you. You will indeed not be caught up in the trap of self pity due to lack of money, now and in future. There are so many people out there who have lots of money, riches and wealth and you should not doubt that they have plenty of things in abundance that will make them live their short lives on earth with fulfilment. Human life came only once to you and its span is quite short, so you deserve to live it with maximum enjoyment.

I have included very important concepts in my book and because knowledge has no restricted domain of validity you are at liberty to explore them further: Child development in chapter 2 and the human brain & mind in chapter 3 are wide and interesting topics. In chapter 4 you will read the perspectives of learning which equips you with the understanding of how people learn and its relevance to acquiring money riches and wealth. Chapter 5 on competition explicitly equips you with the competitive urge and leads you to discover the importance of creativity in chapter 6. The principal subject of this book, Money, Riches and Wealth is highlighted in chapter 7 followed by the thrilling topic on the age conundrum. Then the instinctive chapter 10 on sex desires is rousing! Chapter 11 discusses capital, followed by the topic on opportunities for getting rich and setting priorities in your life and living. Chapter 16 is the definitive topic. It presents the secret of getting rich. I have concluded my book reminding you that God Almighty, creator of heaven and earth, created all peoples in his own image and empowered them to have dominion of all other things he created. This precept empowers you to emulate God by endeavouring to be a creative person as you live on earth. You too, whatever your age, can have lots of money, riches and wealth.

The beginnings

A baby starts off in life with very few negative emotions and therefore fears less. It comes into the world without fear, but for fear of falling and fear of loud noises. All other fears that a child presents are evidently taught to and learned by the child as he or she grows up. Emotions and fears accumulate like souvenirs as one grows up. With such fears the child will start to move from discomfort towards comfort. It is also true that a child comes into the world without a self concept and every concept of what the child comes to be is learned while growing up.

A child's natural state is instinctively being unafraid of trying anything and is indeed uninhibited in its relations with other people and the environment. The child typically investigates and acts upon his or her world whilst getting to know it, rather than being a mere recipient of stimulation. The child refuses to be restricted into a set way of thinking and often acts and reacts to people and circumstances as it feels. Even though the child learns by imitating parents and others around it frequently rebels against set rules and regulations. Children have ambitious minds full of ideas of discovery. They fear no one or thing and they easily make friends, both young and old. Every normal child shoots off from this proposition.

At their early stages children are applauded for just about anything they do and appreciated by the adults. Child, if it goes like that forever, good luck. However, when the child gets older, the focus by adults generally changes from approval to observing what the child is doing wrong and criticising the wrong doings, for good reasons but also for bad ones. Such criticisms intensify throughout one's teenage life and the child thus comes to learn a lot of inhibitive habit patterns. When subjecting the victim to destructive criticism, being told over and over to stop doing this or that, being rebuked, disciplined or matted with other forms of sanctions or punishment, many adults systematically instil guilt, progressively and continuously such that the negative feelings begin to grow in the child and permeate the child's or young person's personality and flow into one's adult life. Negative habit pattern accumulates within the child and later leads to the fear of failure and fear to take risks, which becomes the greatest obstacle to success in adult life. As a dependant the child or young person may have been subjected to such hell of a harsh reality and the negative criticism and condemnation by a parent and other adults can permanently impair a child's lifelong effectiveness.

The result of the impeding influences in the nurturing growth environment is inhibitive for the child or young person leading to the loss of self belief. When such person is asked to do something that entails risk or trying something new or different, his or her instinctive negative reaction is 'I don't know, I can't, or that's impossible'. A person who has been brought up with feelings of guilt feels inferior, mediocre, low-grade, inadequate and undeserving of good things.

Such an individual would even engage in destructive self-criticism and criticism of others too. He or she may end up failing to take risks or continually trying to discourage others and try to make them feel less significant and guilty as well.

If you were brought up decently that's wonderful, but it is nevertheless surprising to note that many a time children from both decent and inhibitive upbringing backgrounds have never had an opportunity to learn how to think differently about how to acquire money, riches and wealth. Their life time pre-occupations or distractions from knowing this truth has made them remain with poor financial and material possessions. So, in order to undo the negative or sluggish thought patterns that a person has grown up with, normally caused by different people and situations, requires a lot of work to realize that there can be a better way. Someone's negative or sluggish thought process can be overcome by feeding the mind with new positive thoughts. But, some people can never learn by themselves even when opportunities for change appeal to them to do so, owing to their entrenched disposition of negative thought process. However, the realisation can be attained intuitively due to exposure to different environments, situations and people. Thus teaching and learning offer a sure way for changing the negative mental set to the positive insightfulness and understand how to see and do things differently.

You are reading this book now and I am pretty sure that you are a grown up person in your teens or much older. I make an earnest appeal to you that even if you can or will not easily forget the causes of your self pity, the persons or extreme circumstances that caused you to be lacking the money, riches and wealth you so badly need, you must forget or even forgive whoever or whatever you think caused your misery in your past. Keeping with such memories can truly be a waste of time for you. This is the wake up call that I am making to you because you must move on. If at all you faced a tough time in your history that inhibited your abilities, it is now the time to think out of your box. It is you, yourself, who should personally, dramatically and practically attempt to emancipate yourself by developing new thought and habit patterns of positive thinking about yourself. From now on you should start believing in yourself all the time. You will do this by thinking, talking and acting continuously in the manner consistent with the successful person you want to be.

What you need now is to change your mental set, the frame of your mind and the way you think. You need to live with a positive mental set for you to make great achievements in your life time. The beliefs of your mental set will shape your emotional energies and your behaviour. A positive mental attitude is an absolutely indispensable prerequisite for success. You should think back to the days of your early childhood when you were totally unafraid of trying anything and completely uninhibited in your relationships with other people and the environment. Except, this time around, do everything fearlessly to the best of your abilities but candidly within provisions of your human rights and governing laws. You have to be creative, seize any opportunity to make money, become rich and wealthy and live a happy and fuller life. Yes, you can!

The Human Brain & the Mind

Your brain, that gray matter upstairs, is the centre of the nervous system of your body. The brain continuously receives sensory information, and rapidly analyzes these data and then responds, controlling your bodily actions and functions. It is the site of your consciousness, allowing you to think, learn and create. The brain is the physical place where the mind resides. It is the house of the mind. Your abilities and desires to be rich are contained in your brain and if you realise, focus on and utilize this truth you shall go uninhibited in acquiring the money, riches and wealth that you ought to.

The mind is the manifestations of thought, perception, emotion, determination, memory and imagination that take place within the brain. The mind consists of five meditational processes of perception, attention, language, memory and thinking which are the information processes that influence a person's thoughts, feelings and behaviours. Any dysfunction in a person's thoughts, feelings, and behaviours is due to a definite problem with one or more of the five meditational processes, the person's faulty information processing.

The mind actively processes data and information to build up your knowledge of the world, making meaningful sense of stimuli in it and deriving meaningful behaviours. Understanding of the mind can help you understand why you are as you are and assist you to know how and why you become what you become. Your understanding of the mind can help you appreciate why and how some people come to accumulate money, riches and wealth. All winners who achieve great success in life are those who have come to know that they actually have a power within them, their mind processes targeted at making more money and have riches and wealth.

I urge you to use your mind, discover the untapped potential in you and transform that personal potential in you into kinetic force and accelerate to enable you acquire lots of money, be rich, wealthy and enjoy your one and only life ever on this planet. Whatever your status, it is what your mind focuses on that determines the outcomes you want. How to obtain money, riches and wealth must resonate in your mind as meaningful stimulus or you will never get it.

Conscious mind

The conscious mind is the part of your mind that is responsible for thinking, logic and reasoning. Your conscious mind performs the tasks of receiving and screening information through the five senses of Sight, Hearing, Smell, Taste and Touch, interpreting the information, and sending them to the subconscious mind for further processing. Your conscious mind will decide how much money, riches and wealth you want to acquire.

The conscious mind operates like a guard at a security gate, it selects and processes information and sends it to the subconscious mind.

Sub-conscious mind

Your sub-conscious mind is the storage room of all your beliefs and memories. Your subconscious mind stores and acts upon the information given to it by your conscious mind. Your reality or the life you are experiencing now is actually a reflection of the beliefs in your sub-conscious mind. That is why it is important to do away with your sluggish thought pattern but continuously feed the sub-conscious mind with positive and optimistic information at all times. To unleash your hidden latent capabilities, you have to tap into your sub-conscious mind power. Your sub-conscious mind power is like a magnet, it attracts things that resonate with its beliefs. So tapping into your sub-conscious mind which store valuable insightfulness of the world around you can bring you ventures of great wealth and make you gain the riches of your imagination. Your sub-conscious beliefs can create your desired reality just like the current life you are experiencing now is actually a reflection of the beliefs in your sub-conscious mind.

How to use your Mind

When you are consciously living, you become mindful of your own thoughts and actions. But, if you keep up with the deluge of information that you are barraged with each day you often find yourself not using your real thinking. On the other hand, your sub-conscious mind is at work all the time absorbing emotions and if it perceives emotions as reality it will go forth and bring them to final outcome, your reality. Whatever your conscious mind conceives and your sub-conscious mind believes in it, that is what you can achieve. The human's mind works based on the law of attraction, moving the desired information in the direction of the currently dominant thoughts.

Given the way both parts of our mind work, it is important to exercise total control of your mind so that you can be able to attract the things you desire. You need to be able to make conscious choices to change and replace the fear-based, negative self-talk and thinking of inadequate capability with thoughts of self belief that are congruent with the outcomes that you wish to manifest, the desire to acquire money, riches and wealth. This ability to consciously change your thoughts becomes much easier once you become consciously aware of your thought process.

Learning

The ability to learn is possessed by every human being and what each one come to learn and how he/she learns it really matters. Learning can instinctively be goal oriented or targeted for specific learning outcomes. Your motivation to learn about how to acquire money, riches and wealth can help you assemble the knowhow of acquiring money, riches and wealth. Learning is the process of acquiring new or modifying existing knowledge, behaviours, skills, values, or preferences.

It is expected that from the age of five onwards children as learners develop enterprising skills and attitudes. They can attain self confidence and belief in their abilities to succeed in whatever they choose to undertake. Arguably, any learner has some evolutionary link with the thought of someone who mobilises resources to make new things happen, who is highly responsive to change, who sees opportunities that others may not see and indeed someone who is enterprising or showing enterprise, or the entrepreneur. This is how all learners would come to understand the world in which they live and how to interact in it. You as a learner in your youthful or adult stage can indeed display such entrepreneurial traits as well. If not, then try to observe entrepreneurial traits from other people and attempt to emulate them.

Learning occurs in formal, informal and non-formal educational setups. One underpinning official thought in education has been the view that learners should experience a broad and balanced curriculum, in which traditional subjects embody the main way of knowing. But, it ought be noticed that for many learners, all the subject matter that can be taught may just be information for the sake of it and can be far from shaping their thinking through life. The subject matter as excess information is easily forgotten. So, what might actually be lacking in the subject content is the learning depth that produces understanding, the element that would transform the subject content into knowledge. The transformation from subject content to knowledge can only be secured if it is clear what it is that the learner needs to learn. If you want to be rich you should learn how people acquire money, riches and wealth.

This text is a teaching directed towards developing skills, competencies, understandings and attitudes which can equip you as a learner to be innovative, creative, show initiate and successfully manage yourself to acquire money, riches and wealth. This is within the context of the responses to the debate in education and its essence of the learner effectiveness. Out there, you will meet academic and professional education. In academic education you will have learned subjects like languages, mathematics, biology, history, physics chemistry and what-have-you which gave you the ability to read, write and work out mathematical problems. In professional education you specialised in a particular field of study and overall it provided you with the learning of how to work for a living.

However, my theme lesson on how to make money, riches and wealth is usually silently or not at all explicitly communicated to many learners in many education systems! Many people often run into financial difficulties when running business activities simply because they lack the concept of how to earn, organise and control the money they acquired. They lack financial knowhow. Financial education can provide you with the learning of how to acquire money, how to use money wisely and how to protect your money. My lesson on acquiring money, riches and wealth has been mostly left out in the educational system. Even those who learned the accounting basics still lack the concept of how to acquire money riches and wealth.

The learning process is a very crucial phenomenon and even though learning may seem basic and taken for granted as a natural process, the root understanding of how learners learn is not straight forward. The extremes of the learning theory are represented by the Behaviourist and Constructivist theories. The two theoretical perspectives are bipolar and imply different approaches to promoting learning and instruction at every educational level.

Behaviourism propounds the general law of learning that assumes that learners are born as blank slates and teachers must inculcate knowledge into them, that learning is typically a stimulus and response relationship with a learner innately responding to stimulus, that learning is largely the result of environmental events which cause conditioning through repetition and that learning is best explained by change in observed behaviour. The educational implications of behaviourism mean that learners should be assessed by observing their behaviour. We can not assume that the learner is learning unless we can observe that behaviour is changing. Furthermore, the repetition of stimulus response habits through drill and practice can strengthen learned habits—practice makes perfect. Repetition greatly increases the odds of making permanent change. Now, as we can see, the learner's internal cognitive processes are indeed excluded from the behaviourist theoretical perspective of how learners learn.

The behavioural orientation of learning has been challenged by cognitive revolution in which the most interesting aspect to the question about learning is what happens inside the learner's head. It is considered that the human brain gets inputs, processes the inputs and gives out outputs. Thus, Knowledge is a construct of human mind rather than innate or passively absorbed. Everyone constructs his/her view of the world using stored knowledge. The learner is considered as a source of plans, intentions, goals, ideas, memories and emotions that are actively used to attend, to select and construct meaning from stimuli and knowledge from experience.

The cognitive perspective thus suggests that learners 'construct' their own knowledge, building it through experience which allows them to create mental images in their head. The knowledge is essentially defined in terms of the subjective mental states of each individual knower. Constructivism emphasizes the learners' ability to solve real-life practical problems and at the primary stage, all knowledge is thus personal and idiosyncratic. We are all individuals with individual differences and we all learn differently. If you use your brains to acquire money, riches and wealth, it is just exactly your constructed knowledge.

But, by insisting on the subjectivity of the individual person's constructed knowledge alone, the cognitive argument tends towards a denial of the possibility of sharing and communicating knowledge among people. Knowledge should therefore not be considered as primarily a phenomenon of the psychology of the individual, but more as the evaluated and compared social, communicative, cultural, and historical phenomenon. If this is admitted, then it leads us to the intrinsically social nature of all knowledge, a common sense that social factors or social influences determine all learning and all conscious thought. Your consciousness is thus considered as a product of the social world and knowledge is defined in terms of the publicly communicated and constructed societal knowledge. It is your reflection in the society that will make you consider your pursuit of acquiring money, becoming rich and being wealthy.

In reflection, it follows that there is not one particular learning perspective which is always the best for every learning situation. Each approach has its strengths and weaknesses, depending on the needs of the learner. Different approaches will be more relevant and appropriate to the learning abilities of the learner. In most cases a combination of approaches will be used by the learner or teacher depending on the situation.

Nevertheless, acquiring knowledge through effective learning requires meaningful, open-ended and challenging problems for the learner to solve, thus allowing the learner to explore and generate both the affirming and contradictory possibilities. Learning is thus a struggle to get beyond existing knowledge. In so far as you share knowledge, you have to make knowledge your own. You do and shall certainly acquire knowledge of your environment by acting upon the world around you. Your individuality and the society are mutually constructed and co-existing levels of life. During the interaction with other people and the environment around you will do things and things will be done to you, as you act and react. On your route to making money riches and wealth you will not be short of learning and the implications of that learning interactively with your local environment.

In any learning setup you encounter tests or examinations along the learning progression. Testing is an instrument that either by systematic procedure or uphazardly arranged is used for measuring and comparing samples of behaviours and revealing the standing of an individual in the group with respect to intelligence, personality, attitude or achievement. The tests and examinations are assessments that are usually intended to measure learners' knowledge skills, aptitude, or physical fitness. They are meant to evaluate the learners' attained knowledge, achievements, intelligence, outlook, attitudes and compose each individual's performance in respect of one's peer groups and thus provide feedback for the learners. Testing is a tool used in selecting those that have potential to succeed and for self assessment by learners themselves. Tests and examinations thus provide a competition platform for every learner. When a learner senses competition, real or imagined, his or her defences kick into fight or flight reaction. Every time a person faces extreme pressure situations, they make a series of seemingly innocuous choices that determine the outcome of their situation. The first choice made is typically the decision of whether to stay and face the difficulty or instead, to turn tail and run. Any competitor makes the attempt to stay and face the difficulty. If he/she chooses otherwise, then even fortune chance can be lost.

In practical life and living we all learn every day and every day living is not short of practical tests or competitions. We compete for resources, money and what-have-you. If you want to join the rich list you need financial aptitude to compete, become rich and remain rich if you have the acumen to maintain that status. You must know what to do with the money once you make it. Knowing how to prevent other people from taking that money from you is crucial, and you should know how long you have to keep the money as well as knowing how that money works for you.

If you want to be financially secure and possibly rich, you need to know how to manage your money in-flow to you and money out-flow from you. You need to know how to make money and have more of it, how to protect the money you acquire and improving your financial data and information. Money spins your daily life and living, without it you may tell me the consequences. So, learn how to acquire money, riches and wealth but also you need to be financially literate. To become number one is one thing and to maintain that position is another. Others can come intentionally or unintentionally get it from you or they may just surpass you because they become cleverer.

Competition

Why do we compete? Why is there competition? Where does competition come from? Well, the formation of animal life suggests that we are naturally wired up for competition. Biologically, the reproduction process takes a prominent competitive urge. When many sperms are released they viscously rush to fertilize an egg which only supports one of them. The egg is a very pretty limited resource in this case and competition must be very stiff! From a lot of competing sperms only one of them fertilizes the egg, and the winner gets it all. The rest of them become losers and eventually get extinct. So, at the very basic level, there is an urge of 'me, myself and I' first. This is typically selfishness and greed and it is crucial because it is about survival or extinction. The winner takes it all! This shortened narrative is typical of what makes us human beings compete with each other and among ourselves, limited resources. We are wired with inborn competitive urge primarily as a survival instinct, otherwise one gets extinct.

Once any living organism starts life it seeks to survive and live on. All organisms, human being included, require resources to grow, reproduce, and survive. Organisms, however, cannot acquire all such resource when other organisms consume and defend it. This is the very ugly onset of competition amongst organisms and rival organisms reduce each other's growth, reproduction, or survival rates. The smarter or more powerful ones usually survive and let others die or they take the lion's share and leave crumbs to the weaker competitors!

Competition indeed occurs naturally between living organisms which co-exist in the same environment. At basic level human beings compete for water, food, shelter and mates. When these needs are not met deep rivalries often arise over the pursuit of such resources. At a higher level, people compete for favours, jobs, advantage, to be the best, to be number one, or to be the most liked. At yet higher level, people compete for wealth, prestige, fame and self actualisation. Such interactions result in a vast array of adaptations for all groups of people and evolution occurs through the differential survival of competitors. Competition causes migration and immigration. Many people leave their homeland because of unequal access to wealth, power struggles for control or just running away from insufficient resources to go round equitably among those in that environment. People compete for resources, territory, location, or a niche'. Competition arises whenever two or more parties strive for a goal which cannot be shared, or where one party wants a lion's share than others parties. Migration and immigration are a survival of the fittest strategy in a competitive environment.

Life and living is normally associated with competition and indeed human beings exist in this kind of void, in which individualism flourishes for the purposes of selfishness, ego, materialism, the pursuit of self, wealth, and status. It's a tough world and it can be brutal! You may have definitely experienced some sort of low level or high level competition of different kinds. That is reality we all have just to live up to it. For example, rich people are generally greedy and defend what they already have, if not they will loose their riches or if they carelessly keep giving out to others what they have earned, sadly, they too would become poor like the rest in due course. But no rich person will give out wealth just like that because all the rich people need and want to keep their money, riches and wealth and remain rich.

So a degree of greediness is human and normal. You will not be the first one to compete, we are all in it! You have to be greedy to accumulate riches or you will loose it and never be rich! That excessive desire to possess wealth or goods with the intention to keep it for oneself is instinctive. It just moves from the basic level of survival instinct to a higher level of egoism. The supremacy drive boils down to the fact that you have to compete with others and if you are going to compete effectively you need to do so from a point that seems your own best advantage. Your best advantage, your strength that comes from your self belief to win is the core of what is going to enable you to survive, grow, expand and develop in good times and in bad times. Everyone, given an opportunity, seeks dominion of others. Some folks launch expeditions of discovery, taking the role of colonial power seeking riches, fame and glory in the new location in the world. They colonize regions and build capital buildings that give them distinctive advantage to enrich themselves and develop their wellbeing. When you move from the basic survival instinct to egoistic self actualisation, you will want status, power, success, fame, glamour and prosperity.

Your rivals are those people that will do their best to take your position. Rivalry is often fuelled by greed, each and everyone's emotional drive to be the best, toughest, or fittest. The rules of the game can change at any time for anyone. So, you have to be prepared to do anything and everything to meet any threat from your rivals. In business, many companies are in competition with at least one other firm over the same group of customers. The collapse of a competitor can bring about great opportunities for those that remain.

Competition has indeed both beneficial and detrimental effects in it. On the positive side, competition is the driving force of adaptation and ultimately of evolution as well as furthering selfish drives for replication. Competition also serves as a mechanism for determining the best-suited group: politically, economically and ecologically. On the negative side though competition can cause injury and loss to some people involved, and can drain valuable resources and energy. Human competition can be and is often expensive, as is the case with political electioneering, international sports competitions, business competition, advertising wars, arms race and creates a widening gap between the rich and the poor.

However, you are in this world not solely to compete. In so much as competition is a means to getting rich, you can adapt, thrive and acquire money, riches and wealth differently! How? Well, by beating off competition itself. You can reduce competitive rivalry by collaborating, pooling your resources with others to create a sector block, although this also is due to competition. Besides, you can reduce rivalry by cooperating, sharing information or sharing access to specific resources. Nonetheless, another important way of getting rich is by being creative. Creativity can enable you acquire more money, riches and wealth.

6

Creativity

I have briefly explored how the forces of competition work out in chapter 5 and pointed out the main things that you need to be aware of when developing your competitive position. But if you are going to compete effectively for a long time, you also need clear ideas to develop your existing scenario and how to get involved with new chances, locations or client bases. Thus you must constantly be scanning the environment for ideas and opportunities that you can turn into money, riches and wealth. You can serve the gap in the needs, wants and demands of your local people and environment as well as beyond given the global village we live in. So, you need to be a creative individual.

Historically, creativity is the sole realm of God. Humans were not considered to have the ability to create something new except as an expression of God's work. Creation was at most a kind of discovery or mimicry, and the idea of creation from nothing had no place. In later stages of human development, the view of creativity as divinely inspired was dominant and the mention of creativity linked with the concept of imagination became more frequent. Imagination became a key element of human cognition. With the increased interest in individual differences and the heritability of intelligence, creativity was taken as an aspect of genius. Today, creativity is indeed a phenomenon whereby anyone and anywhere people think, design and make new things and systems that has some kind of value.

Human creativity arises as a result of a strong need or desires to generate something novel, original, unique, unusual or different that goes to satisfy a need or want in society, as well as for fame, fortune and love. Your energy that was previously tied up in emotional tension for change, difference or innovation can sublimate into creative activity. Creativity is indeed a legacy of the human developmental process which allows you to quickly adapt to rapidly changing environments, including ducking competition and pertains to the reality that we must have passion, commitment, persistence, and resilience. Creativity looks at what else of value can one do or provide. Creative people come up with substitutes, alternatives or a niche' that attract client loyalty to them and prevent clients from looking elsewhere for what other creators can supply and deliver. In return you as a creative person end up acquiring lots of money, riches and wealth.

Creativity is about creative thinking and the ability to drive ideas forward, making your own path instead of following an established one. With a creative mind you offer society a creator, an inventor, an innovator, or a producer in you who is fast and furious enough to earn more money, be rich and wealthy, and society will benefit. Creativity is about getting a unique selling proposition. Once you do something no one else does or has ever done you can set your price for it. You must aim to make something that someone will buy. It entails cultivating a skill to meet a need that is waiting to be met and it will repay you over and over. You ought to do something and make profit out of it. Keep thinking of what else you will do differently so that you will ultimately make a lot more money for your pocket.

If only you can think of being more creative, you would produce more resources and make them available for anyone or everyone to consume, thereby reducing competition for limited resources! Creativity can avail more resources that people commonly compete for. It is thus very sensible for you to be creative and through creativity make yourself a lot of money and become rich. Oh Yes! That is how the rich people got there. They were or are creative in whatever they have been or are doing. Emulate them, challenge them and if you can't beat them join them and you will get rich.

Creativity is a success secret that counts amongst the treasures of many methods of acquiring money, riches and wealth. Creativity is easy to state and needs very little prior knowledge to understand, yet it has a short elegant proof as a way of infinite basis for acquiring money, riches and wealth. However, it is nontrivial and it is by no means obvious to many people. Creativity is one secret that fewer people utilize to acquire money, riches and wealth whilst many others without it remain hindered.

Money, Riches and Wealth

You can get the money, riches and wealth that you want if you really want it. The money, riches and wealth you want can be obtained by earning it, by borrowing it, by inheritance, by marrying into wealth, by winning through gambling/lottery, or even by stealing it (read chapter 11 on stealing though!). Just obey your instinct. All the above are the means of acquiring money, riches and wealth. Take your time, but hurry up and acquire the money, riches and wealth you need or want. Don't burry your head in the sand, because that's poor enough.

All successful people have become what they are because of their dominating thoughts, wishes, desires and aspirations. Indeed all deeply seated thoughts and desires search for outward expressions through which they may be transformed into reality. Success itself is the achievement of what many other people have failed to achieve. So, my appeal to you is that you never quit the pursuit to enrich yourself, keep trying to be the best. When you have acquired lots of money, riches and wealth you will make a success story for others to acknowledge.

(a) Money

In the socio-economic context money is the universal object that is generally accepted as the mode of payment for goods and services. Money circulates from person to person, between communities and from country to country, facilitating numerous interactions and transaction, be it in trade, social enterprises, political dispensations and business activities. Money speaks all languages. Money is a medium of exchange in which prices and values are expressed. Money functions as a unit of account, a store of value, a standard of deferred payment, and a legal tender. Money is light weight and easy to carry when compared to other precious items such as gold. Thus you principally need money to conduct various interactions and transactions in life. The amount of money that has to be paid to acquire a given good, service, or resource of some implicit or explicit value, that is, the money for which a commodity or service is bought or sold is called the price. Prices of resources are called wages, interest, and rent.

Surprisingly, some people often lie and pretend to live in denial of the importance of money in their lives and hallucinate that money cannot buy everything. Yet, living life itself takes money to buy almost anything, basic or essential goods and services you need to live! In the world today, no human being can rise to his greatest possible stature in talent or self actualisation unless he or she has enough money. One must have many resources to use in order to open and spread out his or her soul and develop his or her talent, but unless he or she has sufficient money to buy them with. Money spans across every spectrum of life and living today and having it facilitates our endeavours. Even if or even when you were a beneficiary of charitable endowments, whatever comes your way involves the use of money to acquire them.

Everyone uses money. It is an international anthem, we all sing it, want it, think about it and work for it. Money sees no barrier, it is accepted across the colour of skin, human race, gender, educational attainments and indeed money cares less about where you live, your parents or guardians or societal sophistication. So, regardless of your upbringing, race, colour, school attainments or your gender, money is always welcome. You need money because money is good and money is power. Money is not evil in itself, although it may work for good as well as work for evil intentions! Money is money and any supposition that money is evil is just a fallacy based on twisted logic or faulty reasoning. Money is one of the most neutral substances on earth. You deserve to have money and acquiring money is a fact of life. If you are a normal man or woman you cannot help acquiring money. Others may scheme things against and try to prevent you obtaining the money you want through any form of injustice, bigotry, or prejudice, but they have a limit and they can only succeed in stopping you acquiring the money you want if you allow them to do so. Let nothing stand in your way. You can have plenty of money if you are keen to have it. Remember also that money makes more money, once you have some money you will be astonished at how quickly it can grow.

In order to succeed you need to understand how to do business quickly. Many people struggle financially because they are simply too slow. Nowadays, the faster you make your business transactions the more money you will make. When you set aside money for growth purposes it will surely multiply linearly or exponentially. When you have the money you need or want you can use it in four ways: spend it, save it, lend it, or donate it.

While the creation and growth of money seems somewhat intangible, money is the way we get the things we need and want. Having plenty of money means you are rich. Being rich implies having wealth and being wealthy means having the abundance of valuable resources or material possessions or the control of such assets. Assets may include land, livestock, buildings, money and many other forms of property owned by individuals or social groups.

(b) Riches

What are riches? Riches can be defined as the abundance of money and precious material possessions or resources. Being rich means having an abundance of money, goods, property or land. Riches are possessions of great worth or value. Riches do not only consist of having more money and much material possessions, but of having them more in proportion than other peoples in your community. Riches are the luxuriant, expensively and an elaborate display of possessions and commands an elegant life style.

You have the probability of acquiring riches because you have the equal chance just like anyone else! You can rise from poverty to being rich, from rags to riches and from obscurity to fame. When you acquire abundant money and wealth possessions you will be considered rich. You will have a greater quantity, superabundance, a superfluity of wealth than you need and want. Having such things will serve you being considered affluent, flush, full-loaded, moneyed and wealthy, and thus having an abundant supply of desirable quality substances characteristic of a large amount of choice. Many people are unfortunately too lazy to be rich! Don't follow that flock, think differently and you will get the riches you desire.

(c) Wealth

Wealth is a state of being rich. Wealth is not the same thing as money and money is not wealth. Money is just something we use to move wealth around. Although there may be a fixed amount of money available to trade with other people for things you want, there is not a fixed amount of wealth in the world. Wealth is in the air, in, on and under the ground, in the bush, in villages, towns and cities. Wealth is anywhere and everywhere, it is lying around and indeed waiting to be claimed and those who claim it are the ones who decipher that wealth is there when others don't see it. So it is up to you, open your eyes and see that wealth surrounding you, claim that wealth as yours if you are clever and conscious of the challenge! Wake up early, work hard and do more in a day than most people do in a month and that wealth will be yours.

Nevertheless, it is important to highlight that the meaning of wealth can be dependant on context. The obvious truth is anything of value is wealth. Wealth is that abundance of any valuable resources or material possessions. Your wealth corresponds to the accounting term net worth. It is the value of all the assets you own less any liabilities you owe at any point in time, that is, the value of everything you own minus any debts, measurable at any given date in time. Once the value of all marketable assets is determined, and all debts, such as personal loans, home mortgages and credit card debts, subtracted, the yield is your net worth, your wealth.

Wealth in terms of assets includes those that are tangible like land and capital equipment, and financial assets like treasury funds, bonds, etc. Financial wealth is a more liquid concept than the marketable wealth such as real estate, stocks, and bonds because tangible assets of non-financial possessions may be difficult to convert into cash in the short term.

Age Conundrum

What is right age to acquire money, riches and wealth?

I have met young and old people with great display of money, riches and wealth. The truth is utterly anyone, whatever the age, can get rich. Almost anyone of reasonable intelligence can become rich, given sufficient drive, stamina, creativity, determination, motivation and application of oneself to have lots of money, riches and wealth. So, no matter how sincerely any age related objections to becoming rich are they are only conjured. Anyone can make money and making money is not limited by your age or any other time factor. All it requires is for you to focus on how to acquire money, become rich and wealthy and things will start falling in place as you want. By focusing on getting riches you will set wheels of attraction in motion and prosperity will be attracted to you. You can change your financial and material status if you want and it is never too late to be moneyed, rich and wealthy.

Problem for the youth

Young people keep thinking about the lack of experience, lack of capital, lack of recognition and that they have more or less nothing. They are inclined to thinking and believing that their inexperience hinders their aspirations and wears down their confidence whilst the tragedy of lack of capital has the misfortune of enslaving them to decades of low wages. This premise can be utterly self defeating and the youth need be careful because you may be very wrong! What ever you lack today is most likely temporary. You need to open you mind, think out of the box for there are many pathways to getting rich for you.

Problem for the older folks

The middle aged, middle class, older folks or professionals, you are a people who are grown ups. You may be unemployed and possibly on state welfare benefits. You may be slightly or more affluent, fairly or more comfortable than the youth. You could be having a relatively decent job and perhaps with the probability of further advancement. You may probably be in senior management jobs. Usually you have a decent house, a mortgage, a wife and children. You may have complained or are expressing discontent about being an employee yourself. You may have even thought of self employment by now, starting your own business either on your own or in business partnership. Yet you are indecisive about taking a journey to acquiring more money, riches and wealth. The main reasons why you such clever people continue to work for others is that you enjoy your work and you fear loosing what you have already gained in terms of challenging work, workmates of same disposition, your current privileged status, assured encouragement of job advancement, on the promotional ladder and on some salary increments.

Your difficulty in getting started on the path to getting rich is the fear of risk to your job security and current happiness of your spouses or your children. You indeed fear loosing what you have honestly already achieved more than you desire to acquire more money, riches and wealth. How will you pay the mortgage? you may be asking yourself. Some falsehoods of employment like the perceived advancement on the promotional ladder or anticipated minimal gains have made you fear leaving your job and thus you have been held back.

You too just like the youth tend to infinitely profess that you lack capital. Many people, including yourself argue too that your difficulties in acquiring more money, getting rich and becoming wealthy is their own age. A lot of people think and feel that they may not fit into the paradigm of acquiring money, riches and wealth because they are too young or too old, they do not have enough experience, they may be over-qualified, they are not educated, they have a criminal record, they may be jobless or they may have found themselves in a job where they are tied up to low pay and what-have-you.

The challenge for the youth
As you enjoy your rights and freedoms you should reflect on your obligations, responsibility and contribution towards development for yourself and your community. The challenge for every youth is that society expects you to demonstrate your personal contribution to community development. You must critically look at yourself and discover whether you are part of society's problems or you are part of solutions to society's problems. No society can attain its social and economic development goals without the active participation of the youth.

I implore you not to trust all conventional wisdom because conventional wisdom may discourage your initiative and only offer you far too many convenient reasons for inaction. The youth by far stand the best chance of becoming as rich as you please than the older folks. You have the stamina and energy burning in you far beyond that of the older folks, the stamina that you can utilize to do long hours of work in your course of acquiring money, riches and wealth. You can work day shift, late shift or night shift, working a normal shift plus overtime and still have energy for further daily life and living drama. The attributes of your energy and stamina will see you through physical knocks that would virtually defeat older folks. Your youthful energy and stamina can be your secret weapon in your pursuit of high achievement if you deliberately deployed them. You are ambitious, indeed fearless, and have self-belief. You are not afraid of making mistakes and are likely to making some on your route to getting rich, the mistakes which are excusable, but admit them when you do and soldier on. With passage of time you can come and correct those mistakes.

As a young person you lack experience and you are surely not an expert in any field. This gives you the advantage to easily and willingly learn new things than the older people who have specialised knowledge which make them resist or not easily grasp other endeavours because of their blinkers due to their specialisation. Just be curious to learn and advance because curiosity has led many people into discovery and acquiring lots of money, riches and wealth. Your instinctive knowledge of knowing modern technological gadgets gives you another edge too. Treasure your speed at learning new things, that instinctive curiosity and knowledge and as long as you foster a willingness to learn, you will expand your faculties of adaptation in this fast track changing world of technology. The way to riches will most likely be with many failures at your age but one success, with luck can lead to another. Soldier on, no retreat and no surrender. Just get rich and no excuses.

You should be determined to get richer than your parents or even better than any other adult you may have known to be rich. You have an advantage that you have almost nothing and therefore you have nothing to loose. Nearly all great fortunes acquired by entrepreneurs arose because they had nothing to loose, fortune often times comes by trial and error.

The challenge for the middle aged or old folks, uneducated or professionals

You are the category of people who work for others. You have enough experience to know the companies you work for and the industry you are in. You have learned much and there is little about your company or your industry that you do not understand. You have seen many start-up businesses, watched too many of them and learnt lessons from those that come crashing down and also those that succeeded and are flourishing. You may be even cleverer than most of those business people who are doing fine.

You can surely spot the gaps in the market and your new ventures can grow and compete with those you work for and you can even poach their personnel and indeed share the market with your former employers. You are the experienced lot, brave enough, motivated enough and trained sufficiently well, on and off the job, and have stamina to go for it on your own. You can really see a niche that is yet imperfectly filled by your current employer and other companies or organisations.

If you attempt and fail you can retry or may even go back to work for others. If you succeed you will be richer and become a friendly rival in your industry. Your fear to go it alone and accumulate more riches is your impediment to acquiring more money, riches and wealth for yourselves. Now is the time to consider whether or not you intend to continue making others richer by working for them or whether you wish to become rich on your own.

Just what are you waiting for? It is easier for you to strike out on your own from such a position. You know how it is done and how it can be done differently. Money lending institutions will listen to you when you want capital for a viable activity you may propose to them. Surely, if you dared trying, your chances of succeeding are more likely and not impossible. Well, it may be time for you to wake up! Don't mind your perceived hindering circumstances. There are lots of opportunities for you out there to utilize your talent, stamina, intelligence, experience, or access the capital you need, and acquire more money, become rich and wealthy and even become a better employer as opposed to being an employee. There are so many untapped opportunities out there begging to be seized upon and just because you have not yet come across any such chance is not a good reason enough for you to give up aspiring for greater heights. Keep looking, keep searching and you will soon attract the opportunity to you. There is simply no excuse as to why you cannot start your own money spinning venture to acquire more money, riches and wealth and change your life for ever.

You should attempt to give critique the established ways things operate or are managed. Assessing critically existing norms enables you to find alternatives. Offering critique to exiting status quo of things is the source of creativity, innovation and thus finding alternatives and enhancing improvement. You must have a thinking that there is always a better way. Those who are rich today through their effort most likely made it by looking at how to improve things or themselves through utilisation of the critique that there is always a better way. What else, when else, how else should you do things differently to enable you acquire more money, riches and wealth?

You can start it alone or in partnership. You can partner with someone from another country where there are more opportunities than in your country. Just think out of the box. Remember also that there are possibilities for you to do part-time job whilst you are engaged in full-time employment. You can earn extra income that can boost your inputs into a venture that can earn you substantial sums of money. When you get that opportunity commit yourself and push yourself up to the highest possible limit. Make an attempt at acquiring more money, riches and wealth and do not just let your current situation restrict your abilities for ever and ever until you get older and frail, when you will have less energy to run about in the money hunt maze.

Mark my words you can make yourself whatever amount of money, riches and wealth you want and that can be the end to your insignificant low wage and gloomy low esteem. You can remove the barrier between you and your dreams by seizing any opportunity from the many opportunities that surround you. You can start a business that will change your life. Working for yourself can be the most enjoyable and lucrative option if you want a meaningful career. You have the very best brains and human capital within you. Be positive, you were born a champion, just wake up to the possibilities that are all around you and make a decision to change your life. Seek to be the winner rather than the loser because there is glory in winning and shame in loosing.

Sex desire

The purpose of this section is to inform you that transforming sex energy into another constructive energy can help you achieve many other greater goals in your life time, have money, become rich and wealthy. Over commitment to physical sex contact dampens the ability to achieve at optimum in other areas.

The creative faculty of the mind is set into action entirely by emotions rather than by reason. Emotions control your thinking, behaviour and actions. Emotions have a direct effect on how your body works. You can learn how to live with emotions, living peacefully with them, transforming them and you can manage them, but you cannot stop emotions because they are instinctive. The most powerful of all human emotions is that of sex. The emotional desire for sex is inborn and it is indeed the most powerful of all human desires. Destroy the sex glands and you have removed the major power source of action. This has been proved by castration which makes the castrated animals passive. A castrated beast becomes docile and more compliant as its prowess, the sex drive, that source of energy is curtailed!

The desire for sex contact is so strong that you freely run the risk of life and reputation to cosset it. When driven by sex desire, you develop devotion of imagination, courage, willpower, persistence and creative ability unknown to you at other times. Sex emotion may be controlled for sometime time but its very nature causes it seek some means of expression. When you are very hot and bothered, but sexually unexpressed, having sex can relax your mental bonds and allow you to surge into different status of consciousness.

However, many people have never learnt that the urge for sex can be utilised for purposes other than sex contact only. Sexual desire can indeed be instinctively expressed in other possible ways, namely the expression of sex for the constructive prospective of reproduction and hence the perpetuation of humankind; expression of sex for therapeutic agency in the maintenance of health; and expression of sex for transmuting or transforming sex energy into some other form of energy:

- ⇨ Sex emotions for the perpetuation of humankind are instinctively for reproduction and hence mankind perpetuates itself to avoid extinction. Communities thrive on population and thus the need to keep a growing population. Sex desire directly connects to our animal need to breed and to reproduce, and when triggered, this instinct can instantly overshadow any other rational thoughts in our brain!
- ⇨ Sex emotions as a therapeutic agency are for the maintenance of health. As a therapeutic agency, sex therapy involves the treatment of those experiencing problems in overcoming sexual dysfunction in order for them to possibly regain an active sex life. Such sexual problems may include non-consummation,

- premature ejaculation, or erectile dysfunction, low libido, sexual addiction, painful sex, lack of sexual confidence, or recovering from sexual assault.
- ⇨ Sex emotions, the sex energy, can be transformed, transmuted, released or transferred into another constructive energy. When sex emotions or feelings are harnessed and redirected along other lines, the positive attributes of this motivating force may be used as a powerful force for creativity and hence lead to the achievement that one envisages, in our case this can lead you to the accumulation of money, riches and wealth. If sex energy is not transformed into some creative effort it will find a less worthy exit!

This third possibility of expressing sex emotions is the main purpose of discussing sexual desires in this book. The sex urge is an instinctive feeling. People are more influenced in their actions by feelings than by reason and the destiny of civilization is established by emotions, the feelings. You can transform your sexual energy and access the states of mind that high achievers have. When harnessed and transformed, the sexual driving force is capable of lifting you into higher sphere of thought. The sex energy must be transformed from desire for physical contact into some other form of desire and action, based on your faculty of creative imagination. The transformation of sex energy into creative energy contains the secret of creativity abilities.

The sex desire transformation helps conserve your sexual fluids in your body. If you have sex and ejaculate and lose bodily fluids, you are weaker physically and mentally for a period of time thereafter. Sexual fluid is very similar to brain fluids and it seems if you deplete one the other too is depleted and you will not be of your best physical and mental prowess if you have just burnt out. You normally feel tired and with limited imagination. So, you can conserve your sexual fluids by refraining from rampant physical sexual encounters thereby avoiding wasteful ejaculation and instead internalise orgasmic force within your body, directing it aloft so that it can nosh the brain and cheer up various energy points as the sexual force flows up into the brain and enable you to perform other tasks with dynamism.

Stimulating your sexual emotion brings your mind to a heightened state of awareness and sensitivity. When this state of sexual desire is achieved, maintaining it keeps your mind in a heightened state of arousal and in aroused state you can use your will-power to turn your mind and channel the sex energy to some other physical or mental task that you want to achieve. Thus you channel that arousal and state of sexual lust over to solving the problem or challenge at your hand that need to be accomplished. If you transform or turn your desire for sex into a desire of doing something else, such as working out a business problem, you will solve or accomplish that assignment with prowess.

Ask any sports person and he or she will tell you that when they go into camp before engaging in a competitive match the team management advises all team members to refrain from engaging in physical sexual encounters. If one fails to heed this advice he or she will surely be mated with some sanction or disciplinary action! Why do you think such tradition is religiously observed by sports teams? Well, it is about the retention of the sex energy. Holding back the sex energy in the body helps sports men to transformed and channel that energy into physical strength and mental alertness so that they can be able to display at top level their talented abilities during the competitive match.

By and large, folks who become exceptionally rich rarely do so before the age forty! The major reason is attributable to the fact that younger people are inclined to disperse their sexual energies through over engaging in physical sexual expression. As a result, the under-forties loose sexual fluid which is the faculty of creative imagination and physical prowess. They are deemed to be physically and mentally depleted with melted away strength and limited imagination when it comes to acquiring money, riches and wealth. It is also asserted that the under-forties tend to squander almost every bit of their money income in trying to meet expenses of courting and engaging in physical sex contact and for supporting the outcomes of such encounters. A lot of people have never learnt that the urge of sex has other possibilities that do hold back the sexual fluid within the body. Those who make this discovery do so after having wasted many years when the sex energy was at its height, prior to the age of forty. The discovery of this assertion by anyone is usually followed by their significant achievements of money, riches and wealth.

Capital

Capital consists of money, resources used in making money and people who plan ways and means of using resources and money efficiently and profitably. Capital is a mysterious benefactor of mankind and a source of power. Capital money without brains is always dangerous, but when properly used money as capital is the most important essence of civilisation. Every society is developed through the use of capital. Intelligent people with money, the capitalists, are the brains of civilisation because they supply the fabric of human progress with life supporting products and services. By holding on to the spirit of imagination, faith, enthusiasm, decision and persistence, capitalists are motivated by the desire to build, construct, achieve, provide useful services, earn profits and accumulate riches.

It is really a shame that even though you have had so many hopes and dreams, you already feel you are on the downward spiral and slowly life just kind of wears you down, with no money, no riches and no wealth. You might have had enough of the 8 am to 5pm rat race, fed-up with bosses, no real freedom in employment, or like most people you have no idea how and where to start from. I reckon you have read newspaper adverts for opportunities, looked through business opportunity and franchise adverts, and tried everything you could come across and now may have become disenchanted with what is available or not. You may feel let down by society, blame yourself or your past experience and now consider yourself a complete and utter failure, you have reached very low morale and it is terribly sad. Well, to be honest you are still lucky you are still alive. Many other people started out in life just as low as you have gone and may be worse still than your situation! They re-bounced from there and today they are some of the rich people that you know in your area. Other were blessed when the tide changed and they found themselves standing from rugs to riches whilst some simply struck luck and seized a slim opportunity that came by.

The capitalist society guarantees you the opportunity to provide useful services and to collect riches in proportion to the value of the services that you provide. If you claim the right to partake of the blessings of freedom and opportunity in the capitalist economy you must know the truth that such freedom and opportunity do not and cannot bring riches without effort. You have to use your talent, training, or experience and accumulate money, riches and wealth in large amounts. Remember that the most important capital you can ever get to make you rich is yourself. You are the best, you were born equal you too have the chance to re-launch yourself. You should not loose focus of your very own dream by side-stepping your own personal financial situations to study the larger national, international or world-view of financial management. You may easily get stack in studying complex concepts ranging from national to global economic conditions and financial situations. Even though it is important to have a greater understanding of how money works in a national or global economy, time could be running out for you. Just get back to basics, focus on the core principles and try to put your knowledge of money into practice for yourself.

There are a number of ways of obtaining the capital you need to get started on the journey to accumulating wealth. You get capital through inheritance, marrying into wealth, gambling or lottery, stealing it, by earning it or by borrowing it.

1. Inheriting capital

When your parent, guardian, friend or relative dies, he or she may leave a Will or a form of a Will that entitles you to inherit what he or she has left behind upon his or her demise. He or she will have passed on or given to you some capital of some form that now belongs to you and you may want to use that capital to getting more riches, go for it. Do not just maintain the status quo of the estates you find, try to think of how to leave them better than you found them.

2. Capital by Marrying into wealth

When you marry into money you will have access to capital of your rich in-laws. It really works! Your in-laws can give capital to you. This is a good chance because even when you separate you can obtain capital based on divorce settlement. Nevertheless, this may not be the eventful way to richness as you may become restless and quick to take offence if you think others are sneering, scorning or mocking at you.

3. Win capital by gabbling games or Lottery

If you like gambling you can obtain capital when you win at gambling and lottery games. But the odds are very bad though as the losing streaks always seem to become longer and the winning streaks shorter! It is a very risky and possibly not a good way to get rich! The game of chance is a half probability of either loosing or winning. Lottery is merely a pleasant name for organised racketeering.

4. Obtain Capital by Stealing

All of us claim to owning some money, riches and wealth, even though the truth is each individual merely defends what they purport to believe they own. We are all mortal and when we die we cannot take anything with us. We are all nothing more than consenting thieves and defenders of what we acquire in this world. Each of us came into the world with nothing and individually we shall expire and leave the world taking nothing with us.

However, be mindful about what, when, how and why you want to steal from others who own and defend their money, things and places. Ownership is the foundation of wealth and everyone treasures what they own. Stealing is a case of moral virtues in human societies. The consequences of stealing are uncertain. Indisputably, the thought that the truth can catch up with you will always trouble your guilty mind. You will spend many years looking over your shoulder in fear of detection. If you got caught up, face legal suit and end up incarcerated your dreams of obtaining money, riches and wealth will be traumatizing!

Stealing is bad. Nevertheless, you might become a successful thief when you succeed in stealing money or property that ensures that you have the necessary capital to be rich. History is made by those who often break the rules!

5. Earning your Capital

When you work for others be it in a big company, small business, government, non-governmental organisation or you work on your own, you will obtain capital by earning it. You can work full time, part time, bank work or as an agent and so earn money and save it over a period of time. This may stand a long-term game plan but you will thus have earned the capital you need. Just be careful not to tie yourself in a low paying job for too long because it will quell your aspirations if it happens that you will be unable to save any cash for your spring capital due to little income.

6. Borrow Capital

You can indeed start with nothing and seek to be rich. You can borrow money in one form or another and the borrowing front presents sharks, credit card, banks, venture capital, credit union, etc. There is simply too much money in the sea of lenders seeking too few investment opportunities in the world. Nevertheless, living by the sword of debt also means dying by the sword of debt. There is indeed good debt and bad debt. Bad debt takes money out of your pocket, and good debt puts money into your pocket. A credit card is bad debt because you use credit to buy depreciating items. Learning how to use debt is one of the most important skills you can learn. A loan for investment to make earnings is good debt especially if the earnings to be made will cover your debt payment and put money in your pocket.

Note that interest rates on principal amount differ widely, loan periods differ greatly and there can be and there are predator lenders that you need be wary of. At worst, you may be better to labour as a wage slave than become a beast of burden to a loan shark. It is wise to live within your means. It is not all doom and gloom though, take a chance if you dare. Risk taking is good when probability of winning is higher than loosing.

Accounting Basics

Now that you know how to obtain the capital you need for making more money, you must utilize the basics of managing money and make the money grow. At the core of every successful business, from a corner store to a global giant company, or from sole trader to a partnership, are the same fundamentals of managing money. You should properly manage the money that your business generates and manage the money that your business consumes. Sales - costs = profit. No business survives long when costs of operations surpass sales. You should learn to live within your means. You have to control your spending. You need to know what your income is and what your outgoings are.

You can spend money on assets and liabilities. An asset puts money in your pocket while a liability takes money out of your pocket. Your financial aptitude is about what you do with the money you make: how to keep people from taking it from you; how long you keep it; and how hard that money works for you. If you want to be financially secure and rich you will need to know how to control your personal cash flow. Rich people acquire assets but poor people as well as the middle class mostly acquire liabilities.

You need to manage your money and also keeping records of all the transactions you make is important. Records make you remember what happened; Records make you do analysis of activities; and Records make it easy to audit your transactions and track errors. So, keep records of what you do with money, riches and wealth in your daily activities.

What kind of people can acquire more money, riches and wealth?

Almost everyone has infinite potential to acquire money, riches and wealth. But, take exception of some factors which are likely to exclude an individual from becoming rich. People in poor health and those with severe incapacity usually find it difficult, no matter how clever they are. Also mental handicaps and very old age rule out any serious accumulation of wealth, except by more often inheritance or rarely winning a lottery. So, that leaves the majority of the population, the relatively fit people and I bet you are one of them.

Anyone who is relatively fit, of reasonable intelligence and with sufficient motivation and application can acquire money, riches and wealth and append his/her name to the rich list. All those who are utterly determined to get rich can become rich. If you have the drive or aptitude to attempt getting rich go for it. You just need have the aspiration, draw upon that instinctive burning desire to better your standing in whatever you want then you will be able to attract what you really want. It is indeed not the size of the dog in the fight but it is the size of the fight in the dog that matters. It is important to stress that do not let your colour, sex, race, religion, upbringing, or lack of education block you from accumulating lots of money, riches and wealth. Stop procrastinating and blame no body. Just go for it, just do it.

The most powerful positive affirmation you can use to assert complete control over your thoughts, your emotions and your destiny is by saying "I like myself" and "I am responsible for my destiny, no one else". Look in the mirror and the image that you see is your image, its about you, the one and only in this world, different in appearance, very unique person that ever lived and you only have one humanly life ever. Never underrate or talk down yourself ever. No one is superior to you because we all came into this world with humble beginnings. The most single powerful asset you have now is yourself. If you train your mind to think in terms of acquiring money, riches and wealth you can create enormous amounts. Be weary that your mind can also create extreme poverty that lasts your lifetime if you do not train it to start thinking of becoming rich!

When you look around and study people who are rich you will surely find that they are indeed just an average lot in all respects, having no greater talents and abilities than other men or than yourself. You watch the rich people and you will see that one thing they have in common is they have nothing in common, apart from stepping up and each one of them saying I want some of that, that and even that, ever wanting to claim wealth which lie about unnoticed by many other people. They can be tall, short, fat, thin, dirty, clean, plain stupid, the good and the ugly, the beauty and the beast, you name it! Many people who have great talent remain poor, while others who have very little talent get rich. Talented people get rich, blockheads get rich too. Intellectually brilliant people get rich, very stupid people get rich also. The physically strong people get rich and the weak and sickly ones get rich as well, it is a conundrum. You really fit in one of the descriptions above, but why are you not rich yourself?

Wealth is lying around waiting to be claimed and those who claim it are the ones who get up early, get fired up and ready to amass wealth. You really have to be passionate about money, riches and wealth if you want lots of it. You have to live, breath and sleep money, riches and wealth. If you work hard at making money you stand a better chance of becoming rich.

Lots of people are too lazy to acquire sufficient money, get rich and be wealthy! They are not prepared to make sacrifices and putting in more effort. But compare such people to anyone who is rich enough and you will notice that sometimes being rich require working your lungs out. Rich people have one thing they share and that is their ability to do more in a day than many people would do in a month. The more they have the more the want.

Notice some traits of the rich people versus the traits of the poor people:

Traits of the rich fellows	Traits of the poor fellows
• They have interested in the addition and multiplication of the money they have. • They seem greedy because they ever want more and also they want to protect what they have. • They seem selfish because if they kept giving out what they have then they will loose all they have and join the have nots. • They are imaginative of how to make more money. • They are creative and spend their money on buying capital items that generate more money for them. • They are ambitious and always look for opportunities to make more money. • They have radical thoughts and are aggressive to acquire more wealth. • They are enterprising, always seeking niche's for the market in order to sell them fast and earn more money quickly. • They have great self motivation to make and accumulate more money, riches and wealth.	• They have interest in the subtraction and division of the money they have. • They fail to protect the little money or property that they have earned. • They spend whatever comes their way on liabilities which never raise money to pay back what it costs to acquire them. • They ever seek to depend on others of higher economic status for support than they do depend on themselves. • They are ever trapped in low pay jobs. • They possess what some may call mental laziness when it comes to acquiring more money. • They always want to receive and even tend to actively asking for or soliciting for aid. • They show lack of ambition leading to the lack of initiatives on how to make and accumulate more money. • They are in a habit of self pity, a cycle that never ends. • They are passive and have low self motivation to acquire money, riches and wealth.

It is evident that people do not get rich because they necessarily possess talents and abilities that other men have not. Those people who become rich appear to have characteristics that set them apart from lesser mortals. But the truth is whatever characteristics the rich may have they can be acquired by anyone with the tenacity to become rich. The key is confidence and an unshakeable belief that it can be done. So, a thick skin helps, stamina is crucial and capacity to work hard that people who know you may even mock you is essential! Your neighbours, your best friends, relatives and the rest of your acquaintances will usually watch furtively from the sidelines, half in awe and half in contempt.

Knowledge learned the hard way, combined with the avoidance of error, whenever and wherever possible, is the soundest basis for success in any endeavour. But common sense is not always common to every body. The inferior man's reason for hating knowledge is because knowledge is complex for him which puts an unbearable burden on his meagre capacity for taking in ideas. The myth that people get rich by having a great idea is a very feasible hypothesis, but it is only a partial truth. All of us have had great ideas from time to time. However, it is the execution of the idea that is a thousand times more important than a great idea. Ideas are just ideas and without deed ideas are nothing. You can Learn and Earn only by Doing. You surely can get it if you really want and only if you try and keep trying again and again.

The main reason why you have not already begun to make yourself rich is because you have not taken the step from knowing to doing. Taking that first step has proved to be the most difficult part for many people, including yourself. The step from knowing to doing is rarely taken. So, do it now, take that very first step to getting rich. It is not even a matter of choosing some particular business or profession that makes people rich. Getting rich is not dependent upon you engaging in some particular job or business. People get rich in every undertaking available. You can get capital if you have no capital, get into the right business if you are in the wrong business or go to the right location if you are in the wrong location.

Getting rich is also not a matter of locality. If it were so, then each and every one in certain localities would all be rich. The people of one town would all be rich while those of other towns would all be poor, or the inhabitants of one state, province or district would roll in wealth, while those of another area would all be in poverty. Surprisingly, it does not work like that and the truth is everywhere you go—in villages, sub-urban, townships, cities, whether in America, Europe, Asia, Australia or Africa, we see the rich and poor people living side by side, in the same locality. Often the rich and the poor people are engaged in exactly the same jobs or vocations within the same locality. Now, if two persons are living in the same locality and dealing in the same business, one of them gets rich while the other remains poor shows that getting rich is not, primarily, a matter of locality. What is it then that keeps setting any given set of people who live in the same area with same livelihood factors apart, Why does one get rich while the other remain poor when they have almost every thing similar? Chapter 16 lays bare the secret of how the winner gets it right.

How to acquire money, riches and Wealth

Do not close your mind to any opportunity to acquire money, riches and wealth. Whether being employed, self-employment or both, keep an open mind about which route you take. You do not have to run your own business if being employed might turn out to be the best route for you to take. Some employees get rich through their employment income. For instance, working in the banking and corporate insurance can make you get extremely wealthy due to large commission payments. For others self-employment is the best way to go and make profits. Working for yourself generally has higher earning potential when you are in the right business and at the right time with right demand for your services. Self employment is a lot easier, flexible and much more fun than working for others. But you may also be worse off than being employed if your business contracts dry up. Balancing the act is crucial.

Using your talent in sport, music or any other forms of art can make you acquire money, riches and wealth. Just check around in your region and country or other countries and you will prove me right that having a recognized talent pays handsomely. Footballers, Car racers, tennis stars and what-have-you, well, talent pays.

If you want to acquire money, rich and wealth you may not be looking for one specific career only, except that any career that you may wish to take must just be a launch pad to your destination of acquiring money, riches and wealth. Any job you get should just be used as a chance to creep into it and understand a particular industry. For instance, you can adopt the idea of teamwork in your employment just to help you understand better how senior and junior employees, departments, companies or industries function. But in your secret heart you must be convinced that working for others is only your survey expedition, which should be a means and not an end in itself. Be conscious in your mind that in any company you work for, team spirit is the sticky stuff that obliges employees to unite together whilst employers use it to fetter talented employees to their employment but without having to pay them enough. Commercially, team spirit acts as a subtle handicap and a brake to ambitious individuals. So, when you are ambitious trusting team spirit and not letting your colleagues down is a feeble reason for procrastination when an opportunity comes knocking. Working for too long for other people can blunt your desire to take risks!

If you get promoted that's very fine. Promotion is always welcome as it brings with it the opportunity to earn more but also to learn more of what you need to know, understand and place the knowledge within a greater context for your future purpose of getting rich.

The ability to live with and embrace risk is what sets apart the winners from losers the world over. Just take the risk and hit the road if you are ready, get on the road to getting rich. If you wish to be rich, you must grow mental armour and a tough skin, thick enough to wade off the inevitable giggling and wicked mockery that would follow your unavoidable failure but also to greet the hidden envy that will come with your eventual success. Beware that there is secret pleasure that humans obtain from the misfortunes of others! Sniggering and scorn prior to any attempt to better yourself financially, taking pride during your initial failures followed by envy later when you succeed, are certainties of life that you must be prepared to wade off. When you definitely get rich you will recognise the secret pleasure often enough in the faces and in the body language of everyone around you.

Friends and family members may consciously and outwardly want you to succeed beyond your wildest dreams. But in their subconscious, often without being aware of it themselves, they might be far happier if you failed or only succeeded to a limited degree. It is a selfish world out there! Getting rich means sacrifice and you should confront and harness human emotions. You have to be willing to fail, sometimes publicly or even catastrophically. But, face up to your fear of failure because it is the single biggest impediment to amassing wealth. Convince yourself that you are good enough and be prepared to work longer hours than almost anyone you know. Do not care what the neighbours think.

You must convince yourself that it starts with your approach and attitude to money. Live within your means and if you're relying on borrowing through either loans or credit card to fund your spending on liabilities instead of assets, you are never going to be able to build up your wealth. Such dependency on credit means your future earnings will end up going towards debt repayment rather than adding to your own pocket. If your debt grows you will pay considerably more to owners of that money and become worse off than people who only spend the money they have. Only borrow when all odds will turn a wheel of fortune in terms of profits derived from sensible utilisation of borrowed capital, 'I bought an asset from borrowed money and it is paying back', must be your motto.

You have to cut out wasteful habits by asking yourself where all your money goes. Cutting on unnecessary spending or stopping on useless activities altogether could free up an awful lot of cash. A lot of rich people are disciplined when it comes to managing money. So that's what you need to be. This means setting yourself strict but realistic budgets and sticking to budget, even though it is easier said than done, is the only control of excess spending whilst enhancing accumulation of money, riches and wealth.

Timing is also an important aspect of effective and efficient management of your affairs, there is no substitute for good timing. There may be luck involved but it is often the kind of luck you help make yourself when you follow your instincts and keep persisting. Act with extraordinary speed putting yourself in the right places at the right time and never slow down. Today, the faster you can transact business, the more money you will make. Transacting business to unlimited customers 24/7 can potentially earn money exponentially rather than linearly. Many people are financially struggling today because they are simply too slow. Those who will succeed in future will be entrepreneurs who understand how quickly business and money are changing, and who have the ability and flexibility to quickly change and adapt. Often times, the years of abundance are followed by years of famine and vice versa. Prepare for the bad times and you will only know good times, because in preparing for famine you can go on to become a rich and powerful icon.

Association is a very important aspect as you start the journey to getting accumulating money, becoming rich and wealthy. Who do you associate with? The poor look poor not because they have to, but because they wear a uniform that identifies them so. If they change that uniform they can change their circumstances and people will react differently to them. Those who look weak and needy are treated as such. The powerful ones will strut, look confident and display optimism. You indeed need to and should look optimistic, powerful and confident on your mission to acquire the riches that you deserve. Make dramatic impressions for you to be remembered as somehow standing out, stylish and capable. Dress smartly, dress wealthy and people will assume you are wealthy and treat you accordingly.

The next best thing to being truly great is to emulate the great achievers, by feeling and action, were possible keep them as close as possible. In the community, you have a circle of people you know through the circumstances of your daily living and each of these people will have their own circle of acquaintances, colleagues, family and friends. Tapping into these networks will help you come across more business opportunities to potential. A principle of success is to associate with successful people. You should avoid people who have a negative and destructive attitude, and seek out people who can uplift and inspire you and help you to reach your goals. But, you should associate with anyone who may even be earning an income many times greater than yours, because they are normal sociable people who will go out of their way to help you follow in their footprints. You should associate with them and you will acquire some of their virtues and merits.

You should ask them questions whenever you can, finding out what makes them tick and how they do the things that you find difficult in your own activities. You may find that they had similar challenges to those that you may be experiencing in building your venture. You should find out how they overcame such challenges.

Successful people in different pursuits normally come from different backgrounds, and with different challenges, but all have aspirations and determination. Your regular association with some of this people fosters a family feeling, a sense of belonging to a group of like-minded people who aim for goals. They can help to lift you up when you feel like quitting and can encourage you to greater heights when you are doing well.

Affirmation is one of the most basic ways to reprogram your subconscious mind. It is simply a process of repeating your goals or new beliefs that you want to instil in your subconscious. This can be done in the form of writing, saying verbally or mentally, listening or acting, until the statement is fixed into your subconscious mind. So, repeating your affirmations aloud or mentally; writing down your affirmations; listening to your self-recorded tape; and pretending to be the person whom you want to be by putting yourself in the shoe of someone you admire and pretend that you are that person. Make affirmations such as.

- ✓ I am the master of my life.
- ✓ This is a rich universe and there's plenty for every one.
- ✓ I accept abundance it is my natural state of being.
- ✓ I am naturally enlightened.
- ✓ Infinite riches are now freely flowing into my life.

- ✓ My life is blossoming in total perfection.
- ✓ Every day I am growing more financially prosperous.
- ✓ I have everything I need to enjoy my life here and now.
- ✓ It is alright for me to have everything I want.
- ✓ I'm getting better and better every day and in every way.

You can either write or read these affirmations before you sleep and after you wake up, or record them and listen to the recording over and over again before you sleep. When you listen repeatedly, your subconscious mind starts to believe that it is true. The key to success in affirmation is repetition. Then you will see in your reality that it's true, because of the law of attraction. The repetition of affirmations such as "I'm destined to achieve true wealth", allows you to start your day with a positive mental attitude and it cleans up your sub-conscious mind with positive beliefs so that your sub-conscious is not polluted by all the negative opinions that you hear wherever you are.

The Opportunities to make you rich

The world we live in is full of abundant opportunities most of which you have not and will not come across. So far, what you only know are those which constitute your own conscious and sub-conscious minds. You can still learn more than you currently know but you still will not exhaust the infinite list of opportunities out there.

Some industries are more enticing and glamorous, some require huge investment to get off the ground and some can be made to work at home. Some industries are growing while others are in decline. New and rapidly developing industries very often provide more opportunities to get rich than established sectors, although this is not in absolute terms.

Ideas

All achievements and every earned riches have their beginning in an idea. An idea can make you see things that other people never see. You can get ideas by listening to family members, friends, neighbours and acquaintances, examining your community and neighbouring localities, using your eyes, watching news, reading papers, browsing telephone directory, reading trade press, or browsing the websites. All such sources of ideas can lead to your opportunity of getting the riches you deserve. You can use simple ideas and turn them into loads of cash! Ideas are certainly of immense importance and so keep using your brain and the ideas that you come across will show you the ways of making money.

Take note though, ideas do have consequences and indeed mistaken ideas have disastrous consequences. Particularly, mistaken ideas in the area of money management have produced more disasters than mistaken ideas in other areas of economic thought. The reason for this is that money is at the heart of your activities. Mistaken policies in the realm of money can have a multiplier effect that can spread to your entire undertakings at supersonic speed!

Nevertheless, enhance your creativity. Creativity is based on the generation of new ideas or new ways of doing things. We are all naturally creative and creativity is manifested in a variety of different ways. Treat yourself to a dose of creativity by putting creative thinking into practice in your career or business. Flexing your creative muscle to come up with creative solutions to life's problems is a survival skill. It is an extension of mankind's ability to adapt to our environment. Once you get in the habit of using this skill, you begin to see problems as a fun challenge to your inherent creativity. So, go ahead and flex your creative muscle. Feel yourself getting stronger mentally and spiritually. Build confidence in your ability to cope with anything that comes your way. With creative thinking, anything and everything is possible.

There are millions of ideas waiting to be turned into businesses out there and once you start looking for opportunities, they are not hard to find. Ideas for making money and getting rich can be in the form of problem solving ideas, copycat ideas, or genuine innovation ideas.

(a) Problem solving ideas

Problem solving ideas are ideas that address real needs of people. You seek to launch a problem-solving business to meet two objectives: when the need for your activities, business product, or service is overwhelming; and when your product or service potential users' lives will be made easier or better. You will look for a gap in the market and find out if there is a market in the gap. You also will encounter problems that will alert you to real opportunity. You may need just slight improvements on existing products or services, or you may think of an invention and revolutionary gadgets that can solve real problems experienced by most people.

(b) Copycat ideas

There is no shame in copying someone else's production, but you will be more proud of yourself if you think of improving on the one you are copying. When you study a business, product or service you are thinking of copying, you should always think about how you can make it better. The best copycat ideas take a product, service or business that works in one location and transport it to a new area, especially if it is thriving in the current town that it would work just as well in your new town. You can also take a service or product and offer it to a new market.

(c) Genuine innovation

Creativity is a way of improving existing ways of doing things. You are a creative individual to a degree to which you find ways to improve the way you do things in any endeavour. Every now and then, someone comes up with an idea for a product or service that was not known to be needed but now people cannot live without that product or service. This is original and can be a niche', a money spinner.

Innovation requires thinking outside the box, which allows you to see a problem or situation from completely different angles. Seeing a problem from another angle helps you to challenge conventional wisdom. If you want you can disconnect from traditional methods of drawing a salary, wage or earning from employment. But you can as well create a large sideline income whilst in employment, a side kick income from part-time. You have enormous untapped reserves of creativity that you habitually fail to use.

Setting priorities in your life and living

If you hunt for ants your achievements will most likely be dismal. Hunt for elephants and you will see the great outcome of your efforts. For many phenomena in life and living, 20% of invested input is responsible for 80% of the results obtained. Put another way, 80% of consequences stem from 20% of the causes. This principle asserts that for many events, about 80% of the effects come from 20% of the causes. An Italian economist Vilfredo Pareto came up with the 80/20 rule when he noticed that 80% of the land in Italy was owned by 20% of the people—the vital few. The 80/20 Rule means that in any set of things a few (20 percent) are vital and many (80 percent) are considered trivial. Don't set your priorities on trivial undertakings! The Pareto rule applies right across the board, to both positive and negative actions and outcomes.

For instance, 80% of wealth in the world is held by only 20% of the population; 80% of work time is spent on low-value activities whilst 20% of work time is spent doing things that really pay off; 80% of your profits come from 20% of your effort; 80% of value of the goods in stock is held by 20% of items; 80% of costs is incurred on 20% of purchases made; 80% of your business comes from 20% of your customers, so take good care of them; 80% of time consuming questions and/or minor complaints are made by 20% of clients; 80% of our unhappiness is created by what we do 20% of the time; and 80% of the time we tend to be alert for what is not working and 20% for what is working.

The implication of the 80/20 rule is that you can apply the 80/20 Rule to almost anything in your pursuits. If you can spent more of your time on the key 20% of activities you will be much more constructive, productive and most likely, make more money. The value of the Pareto Principle for you is that it reminds you to focus on the 20 percent that matters. Of the things you do during your day, only 20 percent really matter. Those tasks in the 20 percent will very likely produce 80 percent of your results.

You need to identify and focus on your top 20% of activities and do more of them whilst doing fewer of the not-so-profitable 80% of activities. When the fire drills of the day begin to sap your time, remind yourself of the 20 percent you need to focus on. If something in the schedule has to slip and if something isn't going to get done, make sure it's not part of that 20 percent. It's not only important to do things right, but also to ensure you're doing the right things. Pareto's Principle should serve as a reminder to you to stay focused on investing 80 percent of our time and energy on the 20 percent of work that is really important.

A similar consideration of interest of how you ought to be setting priorities is the project management technique called the critical path method (CPM) in which critical path of activities is developed using critical path analysis (CPA). The technique involves constructing a network model of the project that includes (a) a list of all activities required to complete the project, (b) the time (duration) that each activity will take to completion, and (c) the dependencies between the activities. Using the values from (a), (b) and (c), the critical path method calculates the longest path of planned activities to the end of the project, and the earliest and latest that each activity can start and finish without making the project longer. This process determines which activities are on the longest path, the critical activities and which activities can be delayed without making the project longer, the float activities. A network model for project activity-on-arrow diagram or activity-on-node diagram is usually drawn to display results of the critical path analysis. As you should comprehend, a critical path is the sequence of project network activities which add up to the longest overall duration. This determines the shortest time possible to complete the project. Any delay of an activity on the critical path directly impacts the planned project completion date. So you will put all resources to ensure that project delay is avoided by committing resources to the critical path activities and finish them on scheduled completion date but also working on non critical activities so that they too do not turn out critical!

Delegation, outsourcing, contracting, partnerships with others can help you sort out the critical 20 percent tasks and sort out the activities of the project network and ensure that priorities are tackled according to plans.

The Secret Code to getting rich

Getting rich is a result of doing things in a right way. Those who do things in the right way, whether on purpose or accidentally get rich while those who do not do things in the right way, no matter how hard they work or how able they are they remain wedged with low incomes and poor. The ownership of money, riches and wealth comes as a result of doing things in the right way. Doing things in a certain way enables you to easily grasp the universals of any money generating undertaking.

Doing things in a certain way is the sign of possessing a high Intelligence Quotient IQ score for acquiring riches. The German-born American theoretical physicist, Albert Einstein, was a great thinker and an innovator. His special and general theories of relativity revolutionized modern thought on the nature of space and time and formed a theoretical base for the exploitation of atomic energy. Many are still struggling to differ with what he established after so many years ago. He made major contributions to the quantum theory. Einstein was someone with exceptional intellectual ability and originality. The statistical normal distribution curve depicts that Einstein's IQ score was over µ+3 representing that Einstein's IQ was above the 3 standard deviations. If you possess the acumen of doing things in the right way you can emulate Einstein in thinking and doing things in greater ways! You can make money, become rich and have great wealth by doing things in the right way.

Doing things in the right way is the secret that has four components, namely, targeted thinking, desired intentions, unshakeable belief and execution. When you have a vivid thought of something you need for a specific desired intention and with unshakeable believe that you can achieve it once executed the plan of action, you can achieve that which you want. This is the basis of creativity, innovation, improvement and development. Targeted thinking, desired intention, unshakeable belief and execution form the secret process that can enable you make great achievements and enable you acquire the money, riches and wealth you want or imagine of.

(a) Targeted thinking

Thinking is the highest mental activity present in man. The evolution of culture, art, literature, science and technology are all the results of targeted thinking. All human creation, whether artistic, literal or scientific, first occur in the creator's mind before it is actually given life in the real world. Human achievements and progress are simply the products of people's targeted thinking abilities. Targeted thinking is a tool for specifically adapting yourself to the specific physical and social environment in which you live. Developing your targeted thinking abilities makes it possible to be more creative and constructive. By developing your targeted thinking skills you can make special achievements, become successful, and attain emotional, social and economic maturity. Targeted thinking can enable you acquire the money, riches and wealth that you want if you target accumulating money, riches and wealth through your activities.

Making money and becoming rich starts with targeting one's thinking on specifically identified activities. Your thinking process creates thoughts which are the primary causes of your behaviours in your life, and if you wish your life to be different in the future you have to change your thinking in the present. As a human being you radiate thought energy and invariably attract into your life the people and circumstances that harmonize with your dominant thoughts. You have the ability to control the causes and change the effects to anything you want through targeted thinking. Targeted thinking is the power which can produce specific tangible results that you ever envision.

You can form specific events and thing in your mind during your targeted thinking and by motivating or impressing upon your thinking you can cause the target things you think about to be created. The targeted thinking is a process which when motivated makes you visualise what you want and it will stay in your thoughts as a clear mental picture, exactly the way you want it to appear. Thus, when motivated, the targeted thinking process creates a clear mental picture that you can hold continually in mind.

It is necessary that you should be aware of the errors in thinking. Errors in thinking include partialism, adversary thinking, time scale error, initial judgement, and arrogance and conceit. Partialism error occurs when you the thinker observe the problem through one perspective only and thus examining only one or two factors of the problem and arrive at a premature solution; Adversary thinking error happens by insisting on upholding that others are wrong and only you is right, as a type of reasoning which can be a failure trap. Time scale error is a kind of thinking in which you the thinker see the problem from a limited time-frame whilst forgetting time cycle. It can be likened to short-sightedness; Initial judgement error in thinking occurs because you the thinker become very subjective. Instead of considering the issue or problem objectively, you approach it with prejudice or bias; The error of arrogance and conceit thinking occurs because you the thinker believe that there is no better solution other than what you already know. All such types of error in thinking will block your creativity. Be mindful that you are not risk averse and can easily fall prey to such errors!

However, you become and indeed you can only make what you think about. Every thing you are today and whatever achievement you have already made are a result of everything you have been thinking about to the time. Everything you will ever become will come as a result of the content of your sub-conscious mind. What you become will take the form of your targeted thoughts. Targeted thinking makes you form vividly clear mental pictures of the things you want to achieve and that mental picture becomes known to you as your definitive vision.

(b) Desired intention

All major successes start with some form of definite desired intention. Behind your mental picture, must be the aim to realize that vision, bringing the vision out to concrete materialization. Your intentions in your undertaking might most likely be to address real personal or societal needs by coming up with products or services that would make your potential clients' lives easier or better. Such purpose would make overwhelming appeal for your need to acquire more money, riches and wealth because you would be guaranteed of demand by the clients. The approach is about having goals and aims, then creating the patterns of activities and behaviour needed in order to aspire to and eventually meet these goals or aims.

When you are trying to become rich, getting rich must be the main focus of your personal life. You need to have target that you can aim at and keep your eye on the target of acquiring money, riches and wealth, concentrating on that target without allowing yourself to wonder towards less rewarding activities. Look carefully and focus your efforts where the money is. You can go into just about any venture and still make money, become rich and wealthy. Your desire for more money, riches and wealth must be strong enough to overcome love of ease and make things work. What you talk about and associate with confidently becomes your own self-fulfilling prophecy.

(c) Unshakeable Belief

You must have unshakeable believe in yourself and trust your instincts. Your unshakeable beliefs form a screen through which you see the entire world, and you never allow any information that is inconsistent with your beliefs to pass through the screen. You should convince your sub-conscious mind that you believe and you will receive what you plan to do or ask for. The sub-conscious mind will act upon your belief, passing it back to you in the form of faith. What you believe to be true become true to you. You should not allow distractions away from the goal that you have set yourself.

Whatever you believe with feeling becomes your reality and you will acquire lots of money, riches and wealth if you make these into your belief system. You must have that unwavering belief that the thing you want is already yours. Look at the money, riches and wealth that you want as if they were actually around you all the time, with you owning and using them. Hold steadily to your visual image, with the aim to cause its creation into physical reality. You must keep to the faith and belief that your imaginary picture of money, riches and wealth that you want to achieve is being realized by taking the mental attitude of ownership towards everything in the mental picture of what you want.

Faith is in general the persuasion of the mind that something is true, worth believing in and to assent to the truth of what is declared by yourself as truthfulness. Faith implies a trusting reliance upon future events or outcomes. Thus, faith is a state of mind that may be induced or created, by affirmation or repeated instructions to the sub-conscious mind. Any impulse of targeted thinking which is repeatedly passed on to the sub-conscious mind will finally be accepted and acted upon. The sub-conscious mind proceeds to translate that impulse into its physical equivalent by the most practical procedure available. The emotional part of thinking are the factors that will give your targeted thinking vivacity.

(c) Execution

Execution is the implementation that follows any preliminary thinking so that what was thought of actually happens. It is the process of doing something or causing something to happen intentionally or willfully in order to accomplish an objective. Execution is a process because it has actual inputs, real processes and actual output or outcome. Putting your plan into effect depends on your will power, self belief and your spirit of being a winner. You need to have a no nonsense attitude and non-negotiable appetite to succeed in order to make things to be done by you and any other people that you may involve, according to your will. Taking that first step has proved to be the most difficult part for many people, including yourself. The step from knowing to doing is rarely taken. So, do it now, take that very first step to getting rich. Whilst calculating the best means to achieve your ends you ought to act to maximize the satisfaction of your desires.

You can think of an idea, steal an idea, copy an idea or emulate an idea, but there is no substance having a great idea if it is hard to implement. Unless the idea is executed efficiently and with originality, it does not matter how great the idea is, the enterprise will fail. The implementation of the idea to realise the eventual goal is vastly more important than any idea itself. Implementation of ideas can turn you a fortune of money, riches and wealth.

When starting the creative power into action, there is no room for vague desires and misty concept of what you want to do, to have or to become. By thought, the money, riches and wealth you want is brought to you and by action you receive the money, riches and wealth you want. The vision must set all the creative forces at work in and through their regular channels of action but directed towards you. Your personal action upon people and things will cause the forces in your own present environment to move you towards the money, riches and wealth which you have envisioned. Every day is either a successful day or a day of failure. It is the successful days which get you what you want. If every day is a success you cannot fail to get the money, riches and wealth. So, learn by doing because practice makes perfect. By action you will acquire the money, riches and wealth that you deserve.

Conclusion

God Almighty the creator of Heaven and Earth, made you in his own image and has the pleasure of giving you dominion of the earthly kingdom. God lives, does and enjoys things through humanity. God loves you, God wants to live all that is in you and wants you to have all that you can use to live life most abundantly. It is God who works in you to want, to will, to do and to have. The most important part is to focus your purpose on this earth and express God's desire.

Every form and process you see in nature is the visible expression of God's thought. That is the way all things were created. We live in a thought of a moving universe extended throughout a formless substance and the thinking power moving according to that thought of the creator took the form of systems of planets and maintains that form. So, thought is the most important power which can produce tangible money, riches and wealth.

Since the world is God's creation and since God placed you in such a close relationship to the material world, the creation and use of wealth is a perfectly proper activity. Life itself demands that you be continually involved in the process of money, riches and wealth creation. The basic necessities for living are not provided like manna, for the land has to be cultivated, the sea has to be harvested, minerals have to be extracted, the city has to be supplied with services. God created you with the capacity and the desire to do all these things. Life itself, therefore, demands that you use what God has given you to provide the necessities.

Scripture does not treat either money, riches or wealth as inherently evil. On the contrary, you have a mandate to create and own money, riches and wealth. God placed you in his world to cultivate it, improve it and harness its resources for your own use. You have been created a human being to have dominion of this world. The urge to control, direct and manage the resources of this world is part and parcel of your nature and vocation. You must treat idleness as alien to your personality. God intended you to enjoy his world therefore you should never feel a sense of guilt from living in a decent house, driving a solid car, wearing proper suit or clothes or eating a good meal.

God is a creator and competes with no one. As human being you are a direct or indirect competitor for resources against your fellow human beings on the planet. You should emulate God and harness creativity so that you compete creatively. Creative competition is a way of improving existing ways of living and doing things through diversification which generates more opportunities and resources. You are indeed a creative individual to the degree to which you find ways to innovate and improve the way you do things in any area. When you acquire the money, riches and wealth through creativity, let others around you have more as well by showing them the means of how to get there. Conduct your business such that it will be a sort of ladder by which all around you—employees, neighbours, friends, relatives or all those who will take the trouble, may acquire money, climb to riches and wealth themselves too. Given the opportunity, it is not your fault if they will not do so.

The difficult point with most people is that they retain the bad mentality that poverty and self-sacrifice are pleasing to God. They look upon poverty as a part of the plan, a necessity of nature. That is wrong! You must fix upon your consciousness on the fact that the desire you feel for the possession of riches is one with the desire of omnipotence for more complete expression. God wants those who can appreciate beauty to be able to surround themselves with beautiful things; He wants those who can discern truth to have every opportunity to travel and observe; He wants those who can appreciate dress to be beautifully clothed and those who can appreciate good food to be luxuriously fed.

Get rid of the idea that God wants you to sacrifice everything and yourself for others all the time and that you can secure his favour by doing so. God requires nothing of the kind. What God wants is that you should make the most of yourself, for yourself and for others. You can help others more by making the most of yourself than in any other way. You can make the most of yourself only by acquiring enough money, riches and wealth. Make the money first only then will you be able to donate to charity and continue doing so in future. Nevertheless, it would be wiser for you to promote creativity in those that you help by providing them with the fishing hook rather than giving them the fish itself!

So, it is right and praiseworthy that you should give first the best thought to the work of acquiring money, riches and wealth. Keep reminding yourself that you have a power within you that is superior to any condition or circumstance you may encounter en-route to your goal. Refuse to let your present poor results or status influence your thinking. You are the master of your own destiny and you can acquire the money, riches and wealth when you dare go for it.

May God bless you abundantly.

www.ingramcontent.com/pod-product-compliance
Lightning Source LLC
Chambersburg PA
CBHW030914180526
45163CB00004B/1833